CHALKING THE PAVEMENT

Kate Noakes has published eight collections of poetry and one non-fiction title, and has been published widely in magazines and journals in the UK, US, and Europe. She earned her doctorate in creative and critical writing from the University of Reading in 2023. Kate founded Paris Lit Up, and for four years was a trustee of Spread the Word. She has taught workshops for Paris Lit Up and the Poetry School amongst others, and reviews for *The North, Poetry London, London Grip* and other magazines. Of Welsh heritage, she lives in London.

Chalking the Pavement

Kate Noakes

Broken Sleep Books

ISBN: 978-1-916938-15-1

Cover designed by Aaron Kent

Edited and Typeset by Aaton Kent

Broken Sleep Books Ltd
PO BOX 102
Llandysul
SA44 9BG

CONTENTS

THE SICK SPRING

Thirteenth March, a Friday with which comes
a most lauded play, Stoppard's last contract:
Vienna, and a family succumbs,
fortunes and losses in Leopoldstadt.

I am treated to the stalls by a friend
of a friend, a nice man I do not know.
His cancelled cultural holiday ends
with a short email critique of the show.

I give him scenes, chronology, pictures,
timings avoiding history's clichés;
how I stepped into busy Leicester Square
with foreboding that hurried me away,

and how I scurried home to a semi-death:
headache, sore throat, cough and struggle for breath.

FIELD NOTES 2020

I trace the dark pattern of bronchioles in the branches of a March oak. Leaves at its base, dry as a cough, turn in a sharp wind. Spring is locked out save the singing. I open the catch to blackbirds, robins, wrens.

*

The not-so-busy main road is the distance between us; being me and my dog at the entrance to the park on the one side, on the other, the Polish lady who breeds Miniature Pinschers, and for whom I am sometimes mistaken if people look at dogs and not their owners. I wave. She waves back. Her two dogs sniff at something irresistible by the cherry tree; mine is focused on fox scat.

*

My new acquaintance, Ben, from across the road thinks the poor turn out for Thursday night's applause is due to the nature of the people who live around here. He does not elaborate. I'm happy with the quiet. He enjoys daily bike rides on empty streets.

*

Lounging in the park is against the rules. Luckily my favourite place in the world is my bed. It's commodious and my dog is happy there too in his self-made duvet nest. I've read, written and suffered in it for years. Some days it's hard to see the covering under the layers of paper and books. Some days, like the last twenty one, they go untouched. First light is the best light, when the sun streams directly in my window for an hour or so. Miss that and writing in the shadow of my hand is done.

*

I woke to a damp garden: thirsty plants watered, flagstones washed clean and all those stripy pebbles from Wales shining. I may not be able to walk on the beach for many months, yet bands of quartz in weathered grey hold a promise of the waves. And then, a pair of great tits on the feeders.

*

Stratus, stratus, stratus roof the blue as a crow flaps from right to left across my window. The light breeze lifts the newly opened acer leaves. Children in the garden behind are unseen, but content in their play. The sun is just about to disappear behind the tiles. Day twenty three and I am happy in that way when you cannot go into the world. Hostas unfurling. Croziers of fern ditto. Parrot tulips in green and cream with a touch of red are poised to frill about. The boys upstairs are playing funky music. All is right.

*

The late cherries are more profuse than their early cousins; everywhere redoubled: in the little corner park at night, a white glow of petals under street lamps; in the morning a deep pink overflowing Askew Road by the bus stop. Both playgrounds are barred with shiny chains and padlocks. A council worker stands on the back of a pick up to remove the basketball hoops.

*

When the park was closed for a week, I tried to smell gorse flowers on Wimbledon Common. Today I scoured for native bluebells, found only and only a few, Spanish ones. How I'd love to walk a Chiltern beech wood in its bright green and arching carpet of mauve. A simple weekend trip is non-essential travel, so I must live in the memory of the heady scent of blue, my sense of smell returning.

*

The pink moon is not pink: one night silver, the next yellow, but it is larger than at other times and in that sense, super, and in full view on my night walk, where the usual fox is no more surprised to see me than me him. He stares me out, approaches several paces, then brushes back into the shadows. Bare branches are silhouetted by the moon. Super, I want to bark.

*

Shepherds' Bush Green is a plague burial site. This is unconfirmed, but to this day planning permission is denied. You wouldn't want to be the person to find out, even though you know the infection dies with the victim, or soon after, or so they say.

*

Children are rediscovering, or discovering, the pleasures of chalking the pavement with hearts and messages of love for the NHS. Hopscotch has the thrill of the new, but neither the girl nor her mother knows how to play it. I look around for a handy stone. None are at arm's length.

*

Easter Sunday in Home Park: a mute swan is incubating eggs, her nest huge, the new bulrushes around her, her cob gliding on the dew pond; three black carp sporting; sky larks high above always unseen, but well heard; somewhere a woodpecker hammering; and a surprising kestrel hovering in rosy-blue, then pouncing, his mate on her nest in the hollow of a rotten tree, her camouflage perfect against the cream and brown of the oak. And cherry blossom, fat, pink as our bare arms, cooled only by an imaginary splash from the fountains of Long Water, Hampton Court a mile distant and bright in this unexpected April light. No-one is troubled with anything louder than water and birdsong. Aeroplanes and traffic noise are distant in the memory.

*

The Japanese garden in Holland Park is closed for the duration: a disappointment, but not a surprise. The Dutch garden is approaching its peak: hundreds of tulips, dark and light, their little hearts opening in the blaze, and all the white beds are an attraction and a sadness as I know they will be at their best at night and so, unattainable.

*

Flaming parrot tulips are battered by the changeling northerly wind and I am reminded that their carmine, cream and green stripes were originally caused by a breaking virus in either one of its severe or mild forms.

*

When you've cleaned your house until it shines, the only thing left is to start scrubbing your front wall. It helps that '50s vibe if you are in an apron and have scraped your hair up in a scarf. Puffing runners and sweaty cyclists are under new and specific advisement to keep the regulation two metres apart from themselves and the rest of us. Special notices are at the park gates just for them. I am brushed past without so much as a by your leave, or should that be leave me by? It remains illegal to remove the signs.

*

It took two and a half hours to buy three cans of paint on the B&Q website. When I went to collect them, they were selling plants. What joy there is in a deep pink azalea, and three packets of summer bulbs, which I shall post to my mother, if I can find an open Post Office. That seems to be rarer than toilet paper was a month ago.

*

A new kind of litter has appeared. It comes in two forms and various shades of blue from palest sky to deepest sea: basic surgical masks and gloves; neither of which seem to be at all effective in stopping the spread of the virus, although people are rather keen on them.

*

I am invited to chalk someone's garden wall; a pleasing head-high curve of London brick at the entrance to Ravenscourt Road. A huge rainbow and many hearts and all words of appreciation adorn it. I can't think. Elsewhere a man approaching his one hundredth birthday has raised over £15million for the NHS. The fact that it is not a charity is glossed by the government. I am speechless.

*

Lilacs will take us through the next three weeks. Already in my street its spears of white and mauve are fighting a battle, enemy unseen. Wisteria too fills the clean air with a perfume I appreciate this year more than any, though my eyes itch from some such pollen or just-mown grass. At least the benches in this borough are free from cordon tape.

*

A short walk in Home Park with a friend's mother becomes an exercise in measuring and often sees us stepping off the path over the field of hummocks made by ants; little hills on which an ankle could so easily be turned, not that you would want to go anywhere near a hospital unless you had to.

*

The morning sun on brick: all the earth shades of ochre, yellow and cream, and their complement: the cloudless sky without contrails. Day thirty nine dawns to be filled with activity, little allowance for sitting and brooding. I am not a coot on her untidy nest of twigs. Oh. Wait.

*

My friend's birthday starts with the speckled breast of a mistle thrush, progresses past ransomes, bluebells and cow parsley to the clear brook surprise of a moorhen and her solitary chick. Rebellion is cutting the red and white tape from a bench, or lying a while in the hot grass, or singing of revolution under the new leaves of oak.

*

At first far too much food filled the fridge. We consumed such comfort as can be found in a panic. Half a dozen weeks on there is no need to hoard. We are back to normal, more or less. The French patisserie has attracted our custom though. Flans and framberries at least involve something of a dog walk.

*

Swallows have returned to Longwater; dipping and rising, their white breasts flashing in the sun like the glints of light on the tumbling fountains. Farther off huge carp surface to midge clouds. Cyclists still come far too close and are too lazy to ride on the roads. Three swans flying the length of the lake. How I wish I had wings.

*

The slates pathing my garden are sleek with wet. Dust is
dampened. This morning after weeks of early summer-in-spring
is a change and a good one. I'll rest indoors trying not to dwell
on my friend's friend: two years older than us and dead. All day
the blackbirds have busied about the garden in search of nesting
materials. Such industry, even in the constant day-drip of rain.

*

At first light the blackbirds are already at their nesting. The garden
is singing-green despite the grey. Another day of rain. Another
day of indoors. Another day. It's not that I am fed up with being
confined so much as very tired of being ill. I wish I could see my
family. Phone calls are not enough.

*

A long walk in Esher woods for a galaxy of ransomes and a fix of
bluebells that prove too subtle for me to smell. We gather bunches
of garlic and pick nettles with a plastic bag. A Mandarin drake on
the river Mole is out of place and contrary, but nothing should be
a surprise. We watch him for ages as he ducks in and out of the
overhangs and eventually swims out into the flow. No kingfishers.
A spectacular orange bracket fungus is called chicken of the
woods and is edible. How to celebrate when all of this is over
and we are allowed to park in places where the car parks are not
blocked by skips full of soil.

*

Skylarks twittering through Home Park. I search the air above
in vain, then a flash of white breast or belly over the anthills
and I've spotted one and can now follow this larger-then-you-
might-imagine bird for a few precious minutes. A first. Always
something new. Always something to learn, though it seems the
stupidest coot in London is not learning about the power of water
from a fountain. Ten minutes lying in the sun at Longwater and
I see the world perpendicular – the line of threes, the base of
clouds, the water, all on the vertical; a tipping off balance. The
longer this goes on the more fantastical it seems.

*

Have the blackbirds abandoned their nest? Then, out of nowhere
a flash of wing goes passed my window and I am corrected. It
would be a waste of so much effort if they turned away now. May's
gardens are full of azaleas, rhododendrons, alliums and even early
roses. I bury my face in wisteria and breathe its scent. I do the
same with lilacs. I am mournful and still unable to smell properly.
It's hard to take pleasure in my daily walk. I try to find new places
and keep my face brave when so much is shut away. There is only
so much constant cleaning of the house you can do.

*

My neighbour tells me he's been scaled back to three days a week
with attendant pay cut, yet considers himself lucky; most staff in
his firm having been let go, along with eight percent of those in
hospitality.

*

I chased a stalking cat out of my garden. I hope the blackbirds are grateful. I feel in need of a very long walk, but despite the sun, the wind is very cold. May is indecisive: Friday and Saturday are forecast to be summer, Sunday onwards will be back to winter. I wish the weather would make up its mind. It's as changeable as the government flip-flopping on testing, shielding, and how, or how not, when, or when not to lift the lockdown.

*

I've seen some graffiti – humanity is not a virus – accompanied by a smiley face, all over the notices in the park and the bus stop hoardings for some weeks now. I'm unable to puzzle its philosophy: try not to be defined by this one thing, perhaps; a call for release from lockdown, maybe; more things, what? The pub chalkboard is still advertising the six nations live. That at least brings a smile.

*

A BBQ with friends on their private mooring. We kept well apart. But people, in the flesh and chatting until the dark. London traffic is a breeze: an hour's journey takes twenty minutes, something to enjoy while we can. The eight o'clock clap was very loud on the canal with blasts from all the boat horns and the large number of pots and pans being clattered from the adjacent blocks of flats. The canal is clear, its sediments undisturbed. One might see innumerable guns and knives if one looks hard enough, but there are only freshwater mussels on this side. No shopping trolleys. Blackbirds and robins flew to their roosts right through our party, oblivious; a moment when us humans seemed irrelevant again.

*

I didn't know there were pipistrelles roosting in the eves above my garden. And what a surprise to spend an evening outdoors watching half a dozen folds of black winging across the blue night under more stars than we have been able to see in the city for decades. It's not just light pollution, but air borne particles that must obscure our vision, or so we speculate over another glass of chilled wine. Piping bats, who knew?

*

Foraging the ingredients for elderflower champagne and more nettle soup, we've grown so used to the overwhelming birdsong as to make no remark on the chorus. Will we shrink from traffic and aircraft noise when they start up again? How dreadful. And will we be startled by the pulse of summer: a cuckoo coming in to range so close to London ever again?

*

Bob, 86, came into his garden ducking under the arch of apple trees to a clearing by the wall two metres from us to accompany our lunch on his new euphonium with the mis-remembered opening bars of Abide with Me confused with Ode to Joy. What better with chicken kebabs in a yoghurt, ginger and lemon marinade? How else could we have seen branches, trellis and sky reflected on a silver bell.

*

In the last hour – grey sky, cold – before the park closes, a few people are dog walking, even fewer exercising; in this case dribbling basketballs and shooting at hoopless backboards or taking advantage of the space to practise roller dance. I watch a skilled couple circle and twirl. I applaud and give them praise. We all know how good this feels.

*

Right-wing conspiracy theory graffiti has appeared decrying the lockdown in the name of freedom, and is somehow mixed up with anti-vaccers. How did this happen? Beach and city parties are being planned. This weekend may see idiots being totally stupid. Mad, and dangerously so. I am staying at home and local.

*

My need to see skylarks, green woodpeckers, kestrel, and the swan on her dew pond nest has become essential. No trip to Home Park is complete without them. The swan's eggs revealed for the first time as she stood to preen. How large. How blueish. How long they have been tucked in the warmth of matted reeds.

*

Alarm cries of a hen blackbird pierce my breakfast as a ginger tom approaches the garden. Long lasting racist graffiti in praise of Priti Patel has been erased from the bus stop hoarding. Martial arts practitioners are out early: tai chi and kendo are a slow precise defence, though a genetic problem in the flight feathers of two young Egyptian geese may halt their progress.

*

A windy day for children to learn or relearn the small pleasure of flying a kite. Prescriptions need at least a week's notice and the pharmacist tells me there is some drug rationing. We have learned that a life is worth sixty thousand pounds; in case you're ever wondered And again there is no surprise in discovering that some people believe rules only apply to others.

*

Swallows fire themselves across the sky; bright crossbows; trigger-tight wings. Dozens of them high above on invisible insect clouds. Always an astonishment of agility and speed. Against all odds and logic, the stupidest coot in London has succeeded in building its nest under the fountain. It sits until the hurt of falling water chases it off for a few minutes. I doubt there'll be any eggs, and even if there were, the chicks would probably drown. Finally, the dew-pond swan has hatched her eggs. Seven cygnets and two eggs left cold in the nest, but seven; plenty enough to be going on with. Grey balls of fluff that swim within days. These are the little moments of joy that have coloured this spring; as in a fearless heron, flying low and within feet of my shoulder.

*

We are too late for the Chiltern bluebells, which are all seed-set under wrinkles of dried blue, but take to the shade on a hot day: a perfect dapple of beech and starry grass. I miss these woods in all their seasons, and sitting in a lovely garden with friends, and eating and drinking, and friends, just being with them to share our worries. How hard it is to be alert and constantly living in the now.

*

The blackbirds are working like crazy to feed their three young: ten days old they are all neck and beak, and cheeping for food constantly. We want to get back to normal. We are tired of lockdown, restrictions and being kept away from those we love. Unless your name is Dominic Cummings: a phrase that can be appended to any new instruction.

*

The blackbirds all fledged over the weekend. They stayed for a day on the fence being fed by their mother. From nowhere otherwise-naked-underpants-man with a fag in his mouth threw paving slabs from his stairs down into his garden with such force they shook the studio. All kinds of weirdness and now the US is on fire with rage, again.

*

After three months, my daughter's belly has swelled, so her
progress around Blenheim Palace matched my dodgy knee.
We had a joyful picnic, planning how I can visit when the baby
arrives. And yes, we did hug. Everything is fluid. It is not how
we are used to living. It's unsettling and makes us anxious. Fight,
flight, freeze. We are much too scared and seldom reassured by
the lying government. It's a terrible place to find oneself: out of
control and fretful about today, tomorrow, and everything. And I
still feel so unwell; now with hay fever, which is a new one to add
to my list.

*

Small victories after a week of none are half a dozen eggs and
enough flour to bake a cake.

*

Last week, sand martins, a huge colony on the beach at Wrabness.
Joy was watching them catch flies in a gale. Astonishment was
their navigating to the right burrow. A special sight I have only
had once before. Two oyster catchers on a log: it turns out their
name is a misnomer.

*

Out in the world everything has broken down, as a walk up the high street on a Saturday morning revealed that social distancing is a thing of the past, when it isn't; a café is open, when it shouldn't be, with tables outside and far too close together; basketball is back on in the park as the hoops have been replaced; half a dozen men are doing judo; and, god help us, the shops open on Monday.

*

The weather is on and off: hot one minute, cool the next, fine, then threatening rain. It's hard to know whether to come or go. I'm in the garden for a while with a book, then back indoors to make Boysenberry jam. And as for knowing what to wear... Swallows are not bothered by this and simply fly higher or lower to hunt, pressure depending. Sometimes I think life would be easier as a bird, but not a swallow. There's too much danger involved in voyaging so far.

*

Summer is in its height now and the solstice starts the downward slope to winter. I banish these thoughts with a second flush of wisteria. I need distraction while I await the birth of my granddaughter, who like her mother is born of heat. Fire baby. Salamander. Will her hair be flame-licked red? Or at least strawberry blonde? Titian is the word to use, perhaps. Sweet Imogen, hurry along. I want to cradle you and kiss your milky skin.

*

By day, swallows and by night, bats all feasting on the swam cloud of gnats. Thousands drive long distances to the beaches of England and Wales to practice being social with beer and knives. Come rain and not soon enough. Chase them home and let them take their litter with them.

*

Tambourine man walking across Goldhawk Road playing as if it were a drum. The sound of festival summer, and the nearest thing to it anyone is going to hear this year.

*

Saturday 4 July and independence for one woman in Hampton Wick is the ability to run down the street in foils, her gown flapping.

*

I can almost see the apples swelling in this rain, their cheeks as rosy as my week old granddaughter feeding; plump as the pair of wood pigeons picking at the lawn for worms; ready as the dogs in need of their walk; heavy as my mood in this weather: the day after day never ending winter-in-summer keeping us long indoors. Enough already.

*

Swifts low flying between the houses at the end of the street tap brick in their short pauses; another sight not seen in the city until this year. A dead long tailed tit near the path in the park. I didn't know they were around here before this piece of evidence.

*

I sleep in a room above the owl. Her call for attention is a lullaby, an aubade of hope, unrequited. She does not fly and I tell myself the tale of her broken wing and rescue, but I invent to pretend her captivity is normal and just the thing you hear coming from a market town garden in Devon. Later, I learn great horned owls are alien raptors capable of taking goshawks and golden eagle chicks.

*

Canoeing on river Avon, the highlight was a shoal of sand eels rising and falling; their bright green and silver bodies were needles threading and dropping in the turning tide. I've never seen them before. I've never owned a wet suit before either. It's taken me fifty eight summers to achieve this. Puffin's favourite food, sand lances are also bait in the tackle shop refrigerator.

*

I want my day to always start with a fishing heron and a cormorant drying its wings on the foreshore near the bridge, the tide running out, and the sun brilliant on the water. White stripes on the river path every two metres are a constant presence that it is hard to ignore.

*

The tattoo quotient in Margate is about ninety per cent at a guess, along with a high proportion of daytime drinking and a crowded beach. Social distancing is a concept reflected only on posters. It is sunny and there is simply too much fun to be had. I'm in the art gallery waiting for the tide to reveal another of Gormley's horcruxes. A seagull fills the frame and Tracey's neon proclaims her love for the place. Later I find a little bookshop with an excellent poetry selection. Something for all tastes then.

*

In the dust that was once grass, squirrels feast on an early fall of acorns. Someone has left out a pan of water for foxes etc. Leaf miner moths are doing their worst. At 11pm it is still thirty plus degrees and my neighbour gives me instructions on where to swim in the Thames, providing I have a trailing float to be seen.

*

A young man is trying to mount his bike outside the post office. I stop to give him as many metres as the pavement will allow. A woman walking behind me overtakes an inch from my shoulder. Words evade me, so I throw up my arms. He tells me to check my privilege.

*

The air's been thick with thunder for a week and daytime darkness lit up by sheets and forks breaking to the soundtrack of great rumbling. Yet, the heat remains clammy on my skin. One afternoon a friend loses everything as a freak bolt strikes her house and the fire burns unchecked for thirty minutes. Ten were all she had to grab anything, anything at all – her studio, her work, gone, gone utterly.

*

All the posters in the Tube advertise shows, plays and exhibitions due to end in March, April and May. The city is like a zombie apocalypse and few tourists brave its streets. This is the quietest it will ever be and still open for business. Bring your own coffee though, and make sure you've been before you leave the house.

*

A family hereabouts owns a pig. Not a micro or a Vietnamese pot belly, but your full-grown farmyard sow. She enjoys a dust bath in the park in the remains of one of the lime trees felled this summer. Dogs don't know what to make of her. Some enquire. Most do not. An unmasked youth entering the Tube at Green Park is upbraided by the Underground staff, loudly called scum several times, and invited to be ashamed of himself. Bravo for a large man risking abuse.

FROST WROUGHT SILENCE

31 October 2020

Hallowe'en came and went in a trick of light,
no treats for us, poetic or otherwise.
In earlier years, autumn had been made flesh
in a leafy wreath of apples, starred with bright berries.

If he was there, I like to think Johnny saw
our little parade through the Abbey
and the service in Poets' Corner.
I like to think he heard me read
'On the Grasshopper and the Cricket'.
I like to think he was smiling mellow:
his name writ on marble not water,
the fruitful tribute propped as near
as to his high-up plaque.

SOURCE: A CAR FIRE

All day fine chains of rain silver the windows,
hard to see, easy to feel in a few minutes outside.

Front gardens are my dog walk vistas of wet:
hydrangeas, crocosmia, leylandii.

Ordinariness is Midlands suburbia. There's nothing
wrong with no cold callers, junk mail, free newspapers,

except nothing ever happens. It's safe and dull
and normal, and it is important that one's property

is well-tended: roses and lavender,
grass verges close-mowed around birch trees.

The avenues are quiet—
no difference in the pandemic, then.

My neighbour sends me a photo of our street
in London blocked by police cars

with a wall of flame rising behind them:
orange action and excitement, yes,

scary, yes, and alive for those brief moments
before the engines arrive.

PONIES AT THE AIRPORT

Piebald ponies graze the winter fields
between Heathrow's hangers and cargo sheds,
on the edge of its runways
and by the acres of standing planes.

There are take offs and landings—
freight mostly— and engines
need tuning and turning over.
In this year's clean air, even empty
aircraft must fly every few days.

Behind worn chestnut paling, the shaggy horses
stamp and graze on through wet and fine.
Their grass may churn to mud, but they are there,
ready, whenever we want them.

ON COMING ACROSS JOHN SNOW'S GRAVE IN
BROMPTON CEMETERY DURING A PANDEMIC

Like all good ideas Dr. Snow's map (1854)
was simple. So simple it's surprising
no one thought of it before. We have, after all,
been making maps for centuries.
All he did was plot the incidences
of cholera on a map of Soho. And then
make the connection to a water pump
at the centre of the pattern of dots.

No fetid pile of rotting vegetation here.
So, disease, he surmised, came by water,
not the foul, poisonous miasma of filthy air.
Or, rather, this one did, there being
no knowledge of bacteria and viruses
for another thirty years. Florence Nightingale
had to rethink her learning. She was right
about cleanliness, though for the wrong reasons.

The map continues to find fame,
at least with first year cartography students
and others interested in obscure
backwaters of medical history,
or anyone curious somewhere new
during one hour's permitted exercise.

WHEN YOU HAVE HOPE OF LIFE RETURNING, THIS

A young man is shot for nothing.
Wrong person, place, time.
Walking down Askew Road is to take
your life in your hands if you look anything like
someone who might've been the intended victim,
or even, as it may be, if you don't.

A young man called Alex is shot for nothing and
his body lies in the gutter for half a day,
while people in blue suits comb the street
for anything telling, gathering
whatever that might be into bags
and piling them in a tent.

A young black man is shot for nothing,
the main road is closed for two days,
and Sainsbury's staff stare from the window
as the police do their part from their cars,
disseminating little— Yes, it's a body.
No, I can't tell you how it got there.

A young man is shot for nothing.
A burnt out Range Rover is found nearby.
Information is sought from the public.
Without answers, a mother will bury her son.
No one wants to see the flowers,
or candles guttering in patchy rain.

COUNTLESS PYRES, 2021

There's not enough timber in stock.
No-one could have predicted this need.
Trees are being felled in parks across
this and every city in the land.
Still, demand rises.

Every day, thousands of bodies
are stacked at the edge
of the funeral grounds, each
wrapped in white linen.

All day masked priests work at
fast ceremonies and rapid prayers
till they too are fit to drop.

Impatient families must wait
for their loved-ones' ashes.
One bereaved man loses his temper
to no avail.

Above all this death, smoke palls
from countless pyres, redoubling
the already dirty air.
You can taste the fires for miles.

SOME SUPPORT BUBBLES

Let me speak of a velvet-suited, tousled-haired
Victorian boy sitting besides a Pears' Soap box
and bubbles rising above his blond head.

Everybody's seen this old advert at some time.
The painting is at the foot of a staircase
in the V&A or RA, or it was, except –pop–

this wasn't how Millais painted his grandson.
'A Child's World' is brand-free and it's been
in the Lever in Port Sunlight for years.

*

The sheet music from 1918 has a titian-haired
pale-skinned beauty holding four red roses,
her head surrounded by bubbles.

The song was around in music halls
and films forever —pop—
before West Ham made it theirs.

*

An air bubble in glass is not of much value,
in fact it reduces its worth,

but in glacier ice —pop—
reveals all kinds of useful data.

*

He tells me that for hours he's watched
hump-backed whales hunting off Cape Cod
with their bubble nets.

I'm not sure I believe him, but —pop —
am fizzing with jealousy nonetheless.

*

Pop-pop, pop-pop, pop—
everyone loves playing with bubble wrap.

*

Pop— Monday was bubble and squeak
and the leavings of Sunday's roast.

If my parents had a party, a shiny red
soda stream often came into play,
my father busy with the fizzy.

*

Pop, pop— I prefer the crafted bubbles
of *methode champagnoise*,
and the drier the better.

ACKNOWLEDGEMENTS

Earlier versions of some of these poems have appeared in print and online in:

Poems and Covid ('Source: a car fire'), *Spelt* ('Ponies at the airport'), and *The Canvas* ('When you have hope of life returning, this' and 'Some support bubbles'). 'The sick spring' was included on the Two Rivers Press poet of the month feature in July 2020. A short extract from 'Field Notes 2020' was in the podcast *The Thunder Mutters* edited by Adam Horovitz and Becky Dellow as 'Lilac Elegies' (episode eight, July 2020 https://the-thunder-mutters.captivate.fm/episode/episode-8-john-clare-responses-part-2) and another extract was included in the Derek Jarman Anthology published by the John Hansard Gallery, Southampton in 2023.

I am grateful to all the kind editors of these magazines and anthologies. Huge thanks also to Peter Robinson who was my first reader. I am delighted that Aaron Kent and Broken Sleep Books were able to bring all these writings together here.

This book is for my dear friend, Chris who kept me relatively sane during the first year of the pandemic.

LAY OUT YOUR UNREST

www.ingramcontent.com/pod-product-compliance
Lightning Source LLC
Chambersburg PA
CBHW051741040426
42447CB00008B/1241